# A LADY'S VEINS

### POETRY BY
### POETIZEDMINDZ

# POETIZEDMINDZ LLC.

WWW.FACEBOOK.COM/POETIZEDMINDZ/

WWW.INSTAGRAM.COM/POETIZEDMINDZ/

## POETRY OF CONTENTS

1. A LADY'S VEINS
2. EXCUSE ME MISS
3. SWEET TEARS
4. BECAUSE YOU LOVE HIM
5. ANOTHER 3 MONTHS
6. THE SWEETNESS OF YOUR POWER
7. FANTASY CONCEALED
8. COULD YOU IMAGINE
9. WHEN I OPEN UP MY EYES
10. YOUR TOUCH UNDER THE SUNSET
11. STRONGER
12. YOU MAKE THE WORDS CUM
13. CHOCOLATE

14. GET IT WETTER
15. I CHOSE MY PRIDE
16. NO SENSE
17. YOU REAP WHAT YOU SOW
18. SO EASY YET SO HARD
19. BLACK WOMAN
20. ANOTHER 3 MONTHS (PART 2)
21. SEARCHING FOR YOU.... LOVE
22. CONFIRMATION
23. WOULD YOU DIE FOR YOUR LOVE
24. FROM A PICTURE
25. PERFECTION
26. THOUGHTS OF YOU
27. THE CHARMER
28. BEFORE I DO
29. A LETTER TO LYNE
30. LOVE DAY SORROW
31. FOREVER NEAR
32. IN THE MOURNING
33. GOODBYE

# A LADY'S VEINS

What runs through a lady's veins

Your own beauty could drive you insane

Endlessly searching through hair weave, fitted jeans

Maybelline eyes and an intelligent mind that could bring

the strongest man to his knees

Satin lips and hypnotizing lips still
couldn't fill the void

within your soul where love continues
to miss



Your pain bellows through your
independence

and your plea to be healed of the scars
from yesterday

are felt through your vengeance

You do not trust but your legs are still spread apart

A father's love is what was missing from the very start

Unconditional kisses and daddy's stern warnings were never embraced

Searching for a trace you were misled and deceived just like Eve was by the snake

Still having nightmares from the rape scares

And when you told of the thrust from
your mother's lover no one cared



Your cries and screams were never
believed

You were labeled a liar and a whore



When you looked in the mirror the love
that you once had

for yourself wasn't there anymore

So many stories are written upon your face

A mother's neglect

A father's mistakes


The lack of forgiveness

The boldness to hate


With every tear there's a new chapter

Whether you persevere or not will be the factor

Not many will accept you for who you are

But first you must accept yourself and your deepest of scars



Your hope has dimmed but I plan to once again ignite your flame

What runs through a lady's veins...

LOVE... because love is God's name

# EXCUSE ME MISS...

Why are you willing to give a man

longevity when his only plan is to only have

you in his life but for a moment?

Why do you open you thighs

for a thrust full of lies?

If they taught a class on common

sense, I wonder how well you would do?

Though you may get straight A's,

it's a shame that you fail at dealing with

matters of the heart, which your school does

not teach you.


The money spent on perm, make up,

and clothes to enhance what God has already

made naturally beautiful, only brought forth a man

who loves the enhancements made and whose love

is conditional without a care about your
spiritual advancements.

Don't get me wrong, I'm sure that

you are fine. Thick thighs, big breast,

and I do respect your mind,

but for some odd reason your finger

still remains bare of the symbol of

everlasting love.

Your children remain fatherless

and your heart remains heartless.

Your bed sheets are filled with another

woman's scent but don't point the finger!

What kind of foundation did that man lay

for you?

It couldn't have been much of a foundation living

at his momma's house.

promises made with your heart

in his hand, with all expenses paid

making minimum wage.

And you never once expected

a let down?

The honeymoon is over and when

the sun rose again, you found yourself

by yourself with a one way ticket to the clinic.

A baby conceived from the misconception

of love for lust.

A foundation built on empty promises

and minimum wage schemes.

You're not disappointed are you?

Why were your expectations so high

when the common ground between

the both of you was so low?

They say that love is blind.

So, maybe you should get a pair

of glasses so that you can see the truth
clearly.

They also say the proof is in the pudding.

Maybe you need to get a taste.

# SWEET TEARS

Baby why does your heart cry

Never will I forget the tears that streamed from your eyes

And the cries that echoed through my soul feeling your pain like the coldest of rain

Sweet sorrows with the most sour of taste

And the expression on your face told it all

The day in which the diamond that you
possess became flawed

And just as a diamond is without feeling
it is rare and unique with invaluable
radiance

The comparisons are easily made but
the difference is that of emotion

The pain from which your heart is
broken

A diamond could never cry the sweet
tears of your sacrifice

Nor could it endure the labor of your
body as you gave birth

Or defiantly stand tall when a deceitful
man defied your self worth

Is your heart not as delicate and
precious as a hard stone

Never could it bear the sadness and
anger where your heart has roamed

The lies and sleepless nights

The worries that stem from
motherhood

And the strength that you exerted in the
absence of fatherhood

Not once did I mention the word love

Though I truly believe that it would fit
you like a glove


Maybe that is why I asked

Baby why does your heart cry

Never will I forget the sweet tears that
streamed from your eyes

# BECAUSE YOU LOVE HIM

(VERSE 1)

Why do you talk about him bad

Why do you cry about what he did

You say that you're not a woman scorned

And you will no longer take his shit

You paint me a picture of all his wrongs

Of how he's not coming home at night


He doesn't respect your opinions at all

He curses you out even when you're right


I hear the frustration that's in your voice

But here's the confusion if you didn't care


You're cooking his dinner and washing his clothes

Right down to his dirty underwear

You say he don't turn you on no more

You sleep by yourself cause the drama's so bad

So what was the reason for giving in

To open your legs and give him some ass

(CHORUS)

Because you love him

Even though the love you shared is gone

You gave up your body, your heart, and soul

So how can you say that you've moved on


I know that you love him

You gave that man your trust and time


Even though he slaps you across your face

You still won't leave that man behind


Because you love him

One day you think that man will change

You had his babies and gave up your dreams

Just to realize that he's still the same

Because you love him

The revolving door continues to spin

This ain't no Tyler Perry movie

There's not gonna be a happy end

(VERSE 2)

You both played the games

You both played the fool

Deceiving each other

You both broke the rules

Communication ain't worth a damn

Now you're telling your problems to another man

This wasn't the plan but this is how it goes

Going through his emails

Going through his phone


Betrayal is deeper than the eyes can see

Someone else has been sleeping in between your sheets


This woman she knows the way you made him feel

That the panties you bought were not to please his thrills


And the toys that you play with when you're all alone

Hearing you call his name when you
begin to moan

You think he don't know you have a
brand new glow

And you think he don't know about your
secret cell phone

The way that he knows it's written in
your eyes

And by the anger you shed to hide the
guilt inside

What once was a haven filled with trust
and love

Is a 6 foot hole that years of lies have dug

And you wonder why you can't sleep at night

And you feel like no man will ever treat you right

(CHORUS)

Because you love him

Even though the love you shared is gone

You gave up your body, your heart, and soul

So how can you say that you've moved on

I know that you love him

You gave that man your trust and time

Even though he slaps you across your face

You still won't leave that man behind

Because you love him

One day you think that man will change

You had his babies and gave up your dreams

Just to realize that he's still the same

Because you love him

The revolving door continues to spin

This ain't no Tyler Perry movie

There's not gonna be a happy end

# ANOTHER 3 MONTHS

It's priceless when I look at your smile

Especially when I haven't seen it in such a long while

Maybe it's just me but it seems as if time

stops when I look into your eyes

Trying to keep my composure when

I know that I'm truly mesmerized

The clock starts to tick and time is

winding down


"Can I spend some time with you"

but I don't ask because there's too

many people around


Your provocative sense of humor

seems custom fitted just for my taste


Your every word picking at my brain

and I know that you see it on my face

What am I to say with only 30 seconds
left

I didn't even get a tear drop of what I
feel

for you off my chest


I look into my rear view knowing that

our time together is coming to an end


Losing a breath of hope not knowing
when

I'll see you again

As I reluctantly open the door I boldly want

to ask, "Can I please take you out to lunch,"

But before I can, your back is turned and I

hear you say, "I'll see you in another 3

months"

## THE SWEETNESS OF YOUR POWER

I want to be close to you and I don't care

about the consequence

You keep your distance and keep me guessing

and I love the suspense

Why is what is not good for me
constantly

on my mind


If I could touch you with my passion

and cum inside of you again

then I would rather be dumb and blind


You are my risk

my pleasure

and my pain


You are my lightening

my storm

and I love your rain

I close my eyes and I am drenched

in your illusion

You give me chills though you are not

here and I face the confusion

Should I keep my feelings to myself

Should I close the book and put it back

on the shelf

You have devastated my heart and
ravaged

my soul


Your remorse is bittersweet but forgiveness

unfolds


Anxiety is prying me to throw away the fear

I can live with my sins but cannot die without

you near


I will bathe in my shame and fall from grace

I will burn in the flames for another
taste


God told me not to eat the fruit from
your tree

But the sweetness of your power has
me back

down on my knees

## FANTASY CONCEALED

Is the handwriting on the wall?

Why am I in constant denial of this fantasy between us?

A priceless dream that reality can touch but my eyes will

not open to feel you.

Afraid to take the first step though I desire the first

touch of you.

Why am I concerned about where this may lead

though the mutual fulfillment between us

has been agreed?

Lord only knows the pleasure in the words

spoken from your eyes.

Your body language is all the confirmation I need.

The smile from your lips is like sugar and
I crave

to taste how sweet.


We both have had our taste of the fruit
from

the tree of life.


Still holding onto the innocence that's
gone.


Feeling the tension from the discretion
that's

been warranted.

I can feel the disgust and confusion
from not

knowing what's to be.


I reluctantly pull back, no longer
painting portraits

of clarity onto the canvas.


The flame that once burned has now
been deprived

of the air to breathe.


To share my breath with you has left my
lungs gasping

and my heart filled with dilemma.

Is this right or wrong?

Why did I not proceed?


I confess that my hesitation was by the reflection

of your wedding ring.

## COULD YOU IMAGINE

Could you imagine a night full of love

without my touch between your thighs

Could you imagine my stroke gettin' deeper

as I make love to your mind

Could you imagine the taste of our kiss

and feel the chills run down your spine

Could you imagine me holding you close

Feelin' your heart beat one with mines

Baby you can exhale with me I'm not

a man you need to fear

I'll be there through the laughter and pain

and be your comfort through the tears

You can tell me your deepest of sorrows

and we'll pray for brighter days

I'll be there through the stormy tomorrows

I won't judge you in any way

Take my hand and I'll set you free

from lonely nights you don't deserve

Unconditional love you can have it and my

passion I won't reserve

Don't be scared of reality your heart's desires

I'll give to you

Give you trust and security I'll be your rock

that will never move

Could you imagine a night full of love without

my touch between your thighs

Could you imagine my stroke getting deeper

as I make love to your mind

Could you imagine you'd feel this way
from

the first time we locked eyes


Could you imagine that I'd be the one to
set

you free and let you fly

# WHEN I OPEN UP MY EYES

When I open up my eyes

You're the reason that I rise

And I would die to have a moment with you


No need to get between your thighs

Can you elevate my mind

Get deep inside where no one else can get through

And I will be your sacred guide

Who you can trust the things you hide

And you can cry without no one judging you


And I will hold you 'till it's time

To lift you up and watch you fly

Back to the heavens

I thank God for the view

# YOUR TOUCH UNDER THE SUNSET

Blue moons and sunset skies

The smell of your scent has me hypnotized

The sensual seduction of your lips creates the silhouette

My nature so hard though you have not touched me yet

The sway of your body indulges my thirst

Anticipating the sensation when I thrust and it bursts


The texture of your skin is silky smooth

The rush when I cum from your every move


The taste of your inner thigh is as sweet as chocolate

And when you melt in my mouth nothing can stop it


I thank God for your sacred haven of love

Your touch under the sunset from the heavens above

# STRONGER

The thought inside my mind

I cannot hide any longer

But thoughts of loving you just

make me wanna get stronger

I love it when you're touching me

You love it when I'm stroking you

And when you close your eyes

lets me know I'm gettin' the

best of you

I'll kiss you in a sacred place

I love the way your body taste

And when I lick the sweetest of spots...

The way your body shakes

Let me hold you close

Lay my head upon your chest

And feel secure in my arms while

I gently caress your breasts

And if you want it 'till I make you scream

I'll melt you 'till your body creams

I'll grant your every wish

please baby don't let your eyes deceive

Such fantasies and pleasures that baby

you couldn't measure

Satisfaction guaranteed that I can get

you much wetter

The scent of you intoxicates

The strength of you inebriates


I promise that my passion will last

and deeply penetrate


The thoughts inside my mind

I cannot hide any longer


But thoughts of loving you

Just make me wanna get stronger

## YOU MAKE THE WORDS CUM

You know you make the words cum

I look in your eyes and I want some

The perfect curves of your lips

The way that your bra strap sits

Like red to a bull I cannot resist

Humble and soft but your confidence

I cannot miss

No other woman could make me freeze
up

like this

Every detail of you I admire and wanna
kiss


You know you make the words cum

I know that you're fierce but I will not
run


My soul craves for your heat

Do you realize that the power

within you could make me complete

There's a song within your eyes that

makes me so weak


Anything for you

I'll kiss the tears from your cheeks


Baby I appreciate every inch of you that

God made unique


You haven't said a word but listen to how

you possess me to speak


I'll be loyal to you flaws and all

I'll surrender my life to you and

on one knee I'll fall


Can I become one with you until our last days

Will your love become fearless with mines and

not focus on age


I wanna inhale your every breath

And exhale with my head laying between your breasts


I haven't even spoke of making love to you yet

But if I've touched you right so far

you're bound to get wet


You know you make the words cum

# CHOCOLATE

I'll be gentle when I take it

Softer when you're naked


The moisture when I taste it

Ejaculate my Matrix


So warm when the walls are closing in

Anticipation when the tip goes in


I fiend for your cherry with cream on
**top of it**

There's nothing as sweet as the taste of
your chocolate

## GET IT WETTER

I only want you and nobody else

I wanna touch you as I touch myself

I wanna kiss you

Take it nice and slow

Your bottom lip

I wanna suck some mo'

I have no fear with you

I am your man


You get me harder when you

stroke your hand


I wanna taste the sweetness of

your tongue


Play with your nipples till I make

you cum

(Hook)

I wanna get it wetter

Go ahead and take off all your clothes

right now

I'm on my knees and I won't get up

Tongue kiss your clit until your loves

pours down

I wanna get it wetter

Between your lips you feel me deep inside

I moan your name 'cause it gets better

Now get on top for the ride

(Bridge)

Don't get me wrong…….

My love is strong…….

So move your thong…….

And let my fingers get you wetter…….

Taste from behind…….

Star 69…….

And swallow every bit of me up…….

Don't need no towel…….

I wanna drown…….

Open my mouth and make you wetter…….


Pick up the phone…….

And call Tyrone…….

I'll make you scream "He does it better"

# I CHOSE MY PRIDE

I feel the ice run through my veins

My eyes are red burnin' like flames

My voice is silenced from the pain

But my heart is screaming so much rage

I wonder am I going crazy

I wish these walls would talk to me


But I'm left in tears abandoned

Stranded on this lonely street


Can't fear the storm when the rain starts falling

No umbrella to keep me dry


And the smiles become so blinding

Soak and wet drenched from your lies


With every day I know I'm dying

But His will won't let me die

With every breath gasping for love

That my heart has been deprived

And though I fail my heart keeps longing

Because I don't wanna die alone

But I let my pride run violent

Say goodbye love lets walk alone

Shattered glass from my reflection

The truth is ugly when I stare

The blame I bear is such a burden

But can I question what is fair

Because I chose my pride

# NO SENSE

(VERSE 1)

I'm so alone.

And my heart is so cold.

And I can't sleep at night.

No one to call my own.

Why do I deserve this?

When I'm just trying to make things right.

Shit just keeps on happenin'

and I'm tired of fighting.

I wish things would turn around.

Wish I could keep my feet on the ground.

Please, tell me why am I here?

Cause' I'm tired of falling down.

My problems won't go away.

I wipe the tears from my face,

oh why…

am I getting no answers to why

I feel this way inside?

(HOOK)

I'm tired of holdin' on because

the shit that I've been through

don't make no sense.

My world is turned upside down

and I'm tired of playing silly games.

I'm tired of faking because

the shit that I go through don't

make no sense.

I want to just run and hide

and I'm tired of feeling this way.

(VERSE 2)

I'm so stressed here.

Trying to hold my own.

I can't depend on luck.

'cause the good just turns all wrong.

And I don't have any friends.

I find myself goin' out of my way.

You have your hands all held out.

You wanna smile all in my face.

Where do you run to?

You don't even just call to say hi.

But when you find yourself in need

whose number seems to cross your mind?

My conscious keeps telling me

that it's time that I leave this place.

Because I want to be happy

and never turn back again.

(HOOK)

I'm tired of holdin' on because

the shit that I've been through

don't make no sense.

My world is turned upside down

and I'm tired of playing silly games.

I'm tired of faking because

the shit that I go through

don't make no sense.


I want to just run and hide

and I'm tired of feeling this way.

# YOU REAP WHAT YOU SOW

### VERSE 1

Though I know that God is near I know the devil ain't far behind

And though my heart wants to love you I feel the hatred creep down my spine

It isn't meant for you to understand why I laugh or I cry

Cause either way you're gonna judge me but you can't see that cause you're just as blind

CHORUS

And you don't care

But please do know that the reason for your pain is that you reap what you sow

You toss and you turn and can't sleep at night

You wake up all alone when you turn on the lights

We all have demons behind closed doors

I face them all the time but do you face yours

You wanna receive but you don't wanna give

Then you wonder why your heart is full of emptiness

## VERSE 2

You can put on makeup but what is there is the ugly truth

And you can put on hair weave but selfishness is deep in your roots

You can put on perfume but your smell of arrogance is bold

And though you put on the warmest of smiles you make me shiver cause your heart is cold

### CHORUS

And you don't care

But please do know that you're not the only one with a troubled soul

I'd give you a mirror but you won't stare

You think the world owes you
something with your nose in the air

Well keep on walking

You was never a friend

But please believe when you're in need
you'll be alone in the end

Your heart's desires

Your dreams come true

will never be because the only one you
love is you

And you don't care

But you will learn

That when you step on someone's heart
they'll do the same in return


When you pointed your finger and
turned your back

Someone will treat you just as bad and
when you face the fact


That nobody will listen

Nobody will care

The desperation from your soul that's
seeking love's in despair

Will drive you crazy and you can't hide

What goes around will come around

Surely your spirit will die

# SO EASY YET SO HARD

So easy to damage

So hard to heal

So hard to love

So easy to kill

So hard to accept

So easy to judge

So hard to forgive

So easily we grudge

So hard to hear truth

So easy to lie

So hard to live

So easy to die

So hard to wake up

So easy to dream

So hard to keep silent

So easy to scream

So hard to have faith

So easy to fear

So hard to be leaders

So easily we're steered

So easy to speak satan's words

So hard to speak God's

So easy are the even roads

So hard are the odds

So hard to be free

So easy to stress

So easy to lust

So hard to fight flesh

So hard to remember

So easy to forget

So easy to complain

So hard not to regret

# BLACK WOMAN

I apologize for creating distrust within our relationships.

I apologize for the lies and for allowing my ignorance to keep me spiritually

blind from treating you as the greatest gift given to man from God.

Black woman I apologize for not exalting your existence with my loyalty

and unconditional love when you gave birth to our new generation and extended our lifeline.

Black woman I apologize for not aspiring to be the pipeline

for our children to skyline towards the freedoms that we didn't have.

Black woman I apologize for not being man enough to be

in a committed and prosperous relationship with you and God.

Black woman I apologize for my blatant disrespect and disregard

to respect your body which is God's temple.

Black woman I apologize for being a
poor man with little

value to you because with you by my
side I am rich.


Black woman I apologize.

# ANOTHER 3 MONTHS

# (PART 2)

Everyday... round and round I go

Constantly thinking of this woman I really don't know

The vibe between us makes us feel

otherwise

The smallest glimpse of you and a

wave is the greatest

surprise


As fate should have it we meet again

Our eyes connect and the smiling

begins


"Good evening", as I let you in


"We've seen each other twice in

one day it must be Christmas"


Well then I must thank God for

your presence and I am blessed

not to have missed this

Just one chance to make love

to your mind is on my wish list

I've prayed for reasoning to why

I feel such things

You are the glowing light of

perfection in my greatest of dreams

But now my dreams are to become real

And my words to be spoken without shields

Only if you could imagine the desire

for you that my heart yields


And when you feel my true passion at once

you'll never leave me again for another 3

months

## SEARCHING FOR YOU....
## LOVE

I've searched for love in the wrong place

We all search for love's face

I'm yearnin' for your passion and I'm

hungry for love's taste

I thirst for your curved waist

Thank God for your sweet grace

I've never heard your voice but still

I fiend for a small trace


Embrace every wise word

Your spiritual essence


Lord am I dreamin'

Fantasies of being draped

in your presence


Open the heavens when loving you…


Please take away the pain

I seek your strength and gentle nature

through the storm lies your blessings

Is it far fetched or insane

My faith ever so strong

one day we'll meet and what's so strange

is I don't even know your name

I feel we both take the same risks

The ecstasy I crave to get inside your

secret pleasure

What I'd give for just one kiss

Your value is priceless

Though diamonds come with flaws

nothing comes close to how you shine

when the rays hit

Eternal is the flame lighting the path

as the rain falls

My search for you is endless like

the tears when the pain calls

# CONFIRMATION

How to accept it

To face the unexpected

Where did you come from

My mind cannot reject it

Why does this voice say

that somehow we're connected

Wanna react with my heart

but still protect it


Don't want my kindness perceived

like I'm a scheming man


'Cause in the moment of truth I'll give

my life if you take my hand


Is it the plan from the Most High

I'm curious

I can't lie

Are you the missing pieces

to my blue sky

Am I a fool and just twisted

in my deep thoughts


Are we on the same page

or still a bit lost


Can I embrace you with my warmth

and melt away the frost


This love is free

and it's from God

So no need for cost

I understand the loss of words

and the hesitation


What is the meaning of our meeting

and our destination


I try to calm my mind and keep my

anxious heart from racin'


And trust in God that in time he'll

give me confirmation

your

spirit down


How could an angel from heaven bear the face

of a frown


Let me breathe the air of truth into your lungs

True love from God has no sorrow that could

ever be sung

Baby exhale from the lies described as "rainy days"

You can spread your wings into the sun without shade


I'll touch your spirit

Then I'll touch your soul


I am love

and once inside you'll know


Your heart's desires are not far from the sky

If you believe in true love then don't be scared to fly

# WOULD YOU DIE FOR YOUR LOVE

Which way should I go

I'm at the fork in the road

And though I know you're there

I feel so lost and alone

My spirit weeps in confusion

Will I find peace when I'm gone

Would you die for your love

Would you die for your love

Would you die for your freedom

Or would you live for the pain

Would you die for your love

Would you die for your love

Would you die for your heaven

Or would live life in vain

My voice is so weak

My heart has ruptured in grief


I'm not a child any longer

I do not chase silly dreams


They say the truth makes you wise

But all my truth came from lies


When I think that I'm gaining

The truth is I'm so far behind

I pray for Jesus to guide me

Because I've lost all my hope

What is my reason for breathing

When I just wanna let go

Would you die for your love

Would you die for your love

Would you die for your freedom

Or would you live for the pain

Would you die for your love

Would you die for your love

Would you die for your heaven

Or would you live life in vain

# FROM A PICTURE
# (GOD'S GIFT IS YOU)

All I see is God in this vision

The essence of power in four beautiful black women

I see the angels of heaven in every smile

I see the blessing in walking you down the aisle

You are the queens of our heritage

You make a man complete

Bearing his child

Showing us life and what marriage is


You fill our empty hearts full of hope

You are my missing rib when I get hit

from the trials of life and I start to choke


Your shoulders grace a strength that I've never had

I can't deny your strength 'cause if I did then I wouldn't

last

I can't explain your brilliance 'cause
perfection is hard to

grasp

Your spirit gave me life and you gave me
sight from

a blinded path


I know I couldn't walk 100 steps in your
shoes

I love the strength that's in your arms
that show

your sisterhood's true


You are the glowing inspiration why I
fight for my life

And when I'm feeling hopeless

I look at you

hopeful again that I'll find a wife


The blessing that you are is in scripture

The man that finds you has found the light to be richer


What I see from a picture

# PERFECTION

I wonder what it's like waking up next

to an angel

My vision of perfection

I know it was Jesus Christ who sent you

in my direction

I walk in the dark but I lay in your light

Imagining your kisses that touch me just

right

Your strength gives me freedom

Your embrace is my shield


Your eyes are the gates to Heaven

You are God's perfect 7


You are complete from your head

to your feet


Your smile gives me confirmation that

the sun is in reach

How else to describe your worth

I will cherish your every breath like

my first born's at childbirth


I will protect you and give you an unyielding

love that does not produce pain or hurt

A love that is patient and unselfishly puts you

first


What would you give for this kind of connection

I prayed for my desires and God showed me your perfection

## Thoughts of you

I couldn't help but notice you from a distance.

I tried to focus on the path ahead but with some resistance.

Every detail of you can hypnotize.

The perfection of your curves I have memorized.

Your silhouette I cannot forget

as the sun sets and I fantasize.

Your magnificence and power I have recognized.

How many men have been blinded

because for you they yearn?

If I got any closer to your light would I burn?

I'm still curious to know how your warmth feels.

Can I learn?

You numb my sorrows and free my mind.

So, if I crave for you deeper is that a crime?

Strawberries,

whip cream,

and handcuffs.

Arresting me for my thoughts of you just isn't enough.

I drop to my knees…

Please, forgive me for my sins.

Until I kiss you right there and you

beg for me to do it again.

## THE CHARMER

I was born into a world of liars and sin

but every word I speak about you is true

I study every still frame with sharp precision

your existence in my eyes defines why I've

chosen you

I do not wish upon the stars or live for fairytales

but I can feel your spirit and I'm wishing for you

Though I'm a man I sit and daydream

Creating perfect love scenes

Scenarios of marrying you

Lord please forgive me

Can I cut a slice of heaven

Take a taste

Inebriated from caressing your hips

Couldn't create you any better

from your cocoa brown skin

I see the God in you and He didn't miss

You are my hour glass of bliss and if the

time permits

I'll cradle every inch if you don't mind where

I kiss

The fragrance of your silky long hair

Your smile

It has me open

Close my eyes and let the passion commence


And I don't care about the distance

You're my vision

There's no mission that is greater than your

love that I seek


Lets find a reverend that can capture every

vow down to perfection

My expressions through the words that

are

preached


Baby forgive me if I'm moving too fast

but if I blink I feel I'll miss the greatest

joy in my life


If I'm a charmer then I hope that I'm the

best

at what I'm doing to influence you to

become

my wife

# BEFORE I DO…. (I WOULD SAY THIS TO YOU)

You look so alluring in that skirt

From head to toe you are God's perfect work


You send me in a trance with every smile

Your caramel rich complexion drives me wild

Can I run my fingers through your hair

Can I hold your hand and adore you
with my stare


I bet you're sweeter than any fruit I
could ever taste

Give me your seeds of love

I can see 'em in your face


Let me caress your energy

There's love within every trace


Can I be one with you as my hands glide

around your waist

I wanna know who you are

Can you take me to that place

And my patience is golden because

you're worth the wait

I would travel across the world to be with you

We can talk for hours and I will pray with you

I wanna take your hand in faith and loyalty

I wanna be your freedom

Will you marry me

These are my deepest of thoughts that I keep

under lock and key

This is my soundtrack to you and it plays like

a symphony

If the time ever comes and I can connect with you

I'll tell you all of these things before I
put this ring on you

## A LETTER TO LYNE....
## FROM THE SKY

I want you to know that you shine so bright

You are the sun but I understand that on certain

days lightening will strike

From a distance I feel your thunder

It saddens me when you shed your

tears and unleash the rain

You are a miracle from the sky

but you still feel pain

I have compassion for you

and I pray for these storms to pass through

Because I miss the strength

energy and hope that you've given me

when your sky turns blue

You give the world light

And there are some who don't

appreciate you


Until you go down at night

and they are lost without you


When I'm sitting in the dark

I'm praying that you rise again

When I inhale I need your wind


Do you know how close to Heaven

you really are

Do you really believe that the devil

wants you that close to a star


Your magnificence comes with a price

oh so high


But you are an invaluable masterpiece

from the sky

## LOVE DAY SORROW

There is no reason for a smile

Been down this road for quite

a while

When you come around I feel so cold

The more I speak of you I feel more alone

My appetite's gone and I cannot eat

Don't want the taste of your kiss

because

it ain't that sweet

A red candy shaped heart was found

in the batch

Deep inside of my chest is a black one

to match

You toss up my love but you cannot catch

You wanna burn my soul

then just light the match

You can find my face right next to fool

I wanna swim in love but not drown in

the pool


So it's best that I keep my feet on the ground

But my fatal flaws keep knocking me down


I'm not sure if there's love for me tomorrow

But what I feel for the moment is love day

sorrow

# FOREVER NEAR

I looked in the sky today and I didn't realize

That the doors of heaven opened for an angel in the sky

I did not understand why the sun was so bright

But it was Jesus guiding you from such a long and painful fight

But now you can spread your wings

And you can sing songs of praise and joy


Rejoice in Him because you're free

Living in God's perfect harmony


And pick flowers of gold for your hair

And be at peace cause the angels are there


And you can skip through the garden of love

Embrace the rays from the heaven above

And eat of fruit that will fill your soul

Enjoy the sweetness of wisdom's bowl


I know that now you can rest your eyes

Without no worries or sorrows


Say your goodbyes to the ways of the world

It wasn't worth anymore tomorrows


So now today you have met His promise

There is no need to ever fear

You are a Queen in God's Kingdom

Shall your peace be forever near

# IN THE MOURNING

## VERSE 1

In the mourning I'll be with you when
the tears are in your eyes

When the pain seems never ending and
you feel like you could die


Peoples words do not console you and
the hugs don't satisfy

And when they say that it'll be okay I
know it seems like it's a lie

What do you do when the rain starts to
falling and the blue sky turns to gray

No one can answer

It's not their child going to their grave


The devastation runs through your soul
and now your spirit's lost it's faith

You say goodbye for the very last time
your broken heart can be replaced


Chorus


But I'll be there through your darkest
hour

When no one's there you can count on me

I'll never forsake you whenever you stumble

I'll give you the strength but you must believe


Cause in the mourning I know you're weary

But have no fear and I'll set you free


I hear your prayers and I know your sorrow

I'll heal your pain just trust in me

## Verse 2

I can understand feeling hatred when your world's turned upside down

Can't even look at yourself in the mirror and you blame yourself somehow

With every breath there's a struggle within to find the strength to carry on

How to escape from the sins of tomorrow when the love you had is gone

And though this world doesn't care nothing 'bout you there is only one you need

Just when you thought that you couldn't rise again then Jesus brought you off your knees


Just pray to God for salvation and guidance through His Words you will find peace

There is no storm that can ever take you under but you have to just believe

## Chorus

That I'll be there through your darkest hour

When no one cares you can call on me


I'll never forsake you whenever you stumble

I'll give you the strength but you must believe


Cause in the mourning I know you're weary

But have no fear and I'll set you free

I hear your prayers and I know your sorrows

I'll heal your pain just trust in me

# GOODBYE

Not sure if heaven's meant for me

I'm scared when I close my eyes

And though I'm down on my knees

My faith feels so paralyzed

Nowhere to run to

I know I cannot hide

I look in the mirror

I'm stripped of all my pride

You can kill what's left of me

My veins filled with so much sin

My tears cannot save me

or turn my sky blue again

But Jesus I tried…….

And I apologize…….

And if it's my time…..

Goodbye

Will somebody mourn for me

through my imperfections


Does the past consume your heart

cause I lost my direction


Am I worth your forgiveness now

what goes around comes around


I wish I could change my ways

but I know that it's too late

I'd give my life to you

That's all that I have to give


No longer wish for childish dreams

I've prayed but I cannot win


But Jesus I tried…….

And I apologize…….


And if it's my time…….


Goodbye

Look over my shoulders

There's hate everywhere I turn

My heart is so scared to love

The risk is too much I've learned

That I'm better off all alone

And I can do bad on my own

What did you gain from your lies

You broke my heart but that's alright

You can kill what's left of me

I have nothing left to give


Though some days were filled with rain

The sun always rose again


And Jesus I tried.......

Oh Jesus how I've tried.......


But if it's my time.....


Goodbye

www.ingramcontent.com/pod-product-compliance
Lightning Source LLC
LaVergne TN
LVHW051602070426
835507LV00021B/2728